Asotamâkêwin-

Cree Meaning:

Sacred vow that one makes / Promise

Copyright © 2024 by Saskatoon Sâkâstêw Horse.

All rights reserved. No part of this publication may be reproduced, distributed or transmitted in any form or by any means, including photo copying, recording, or other electronic or mechanical methods, with out the prior written permission of the publisher, except in the case of brief quotations embodied in critical reviews and certain other non commercial uses permitted by copyright law.

For permission requests, write to the author, at: saskatoon_horse@hotmail.com.

Author Name

Saskatoon Sâkâstêw Horse

Publisher Name

Sâkâstêw

Asotamâkêwin / Saskatoon Sâkâstêw Horse —rst ed.

Dedicated to The Greats,
My children who are the future.

The moment I became a mother, I knew in my heart that it was time...
Asotamâkêwin
Sacred Vow That One Makes / Promise.

My Washington Park Love Story

In Loving Memory of my parents
Our guiding lights "up the sky" until we meet again.

&

For you.

Kisâkihitin-I Love you.

A sacred space for you to explore the depths of your own journey towards healing and understanding the intergenerational legacy that shapes your life.
Through introspection, storytelling, and self-discovery, you will uncover the threads that connect you to your ancestors and illuminate the path towards healing.
Remember, this journey is uniquely yours, and this journal is your companion in unraveling the layers of your past, embracing the present, and creating a future filled with healing and longevity for generations to come.
These are the questions I began to ask myself and tools I continue to use on my intergenerational healing journey in hopes to serve as a guide for others who are on a similar path.
Remember you are not alone.

Elders Acknowledgement— Asotamâkêwin
A-so-the-ma-kay-win

"We were promised, everybody's been promised.
Whatever we choose, so that we can have a good life."

-Maria Linklater

PERMISSION SLIP

By signing below, you grant yourself:

Asotamâkêwin

Wander into the Uncharted Territories
Explore uncharted emotional landscapes and express yourself freely without judgment.

Dance with Creativity
Allow your thoughts to dance on the pages, Reinventing your own story.

Travel Through Time
Move freely between past, present, and future reflections, discovering the wisdom that lies in each moment.

Embrace Vulnerability
Give yourself permission to be vulnerable and authentic in your self-reflection.

Celebrate Small Wins
Acknowledge and celebrate even the smallest victories and moments.

Honor Your Path
The good, the bad and the ugly.
Nobody is you, that is your Super Power.

By signing this permission slip, you are officially granting yourself the Sacred Vow That One Makes to make the most of every page, unearthing the sacred treasures that lie within your thoughts and experiences.

Signature: _____

Date: _____

Why Write Things Down?

Research suggests that the act of writing has profound effects on our mental and emotional well-being.
By putting your thoughts, feelings, and experiences into words, you initiate a process of self-reflection and emotional release.

The journal becomes a sacred space for expression, enabling you to gain insights, break patterns, and regenerate healing across generations.
Begin your transformative journey today.

With gratitude for your courage,

Asotamâkêwin

5 Healing Affirmations for Intergenerational Healing

I release the pain of past generations and choose to create a brighter future for myself and those to come.

I am worthy of love and healing, regardless of any trauma or generational patterns that may have affected me.

I am capable of breaking the cycle of generational trauma and creating a positive legacy for future generations.

I choose to approach my healing journey with compassion and patience, knowing that it may take time and effort to overcome past wounds.

I trust in my own resilience and ability to heal, and I am grateful for the support and love of those around me who are also committed to intergenerational healing.

Asotamâkêwin

"At our most vulnerable, we unearth an unparalleled strength—the raw power that transforms wounds into wings."

We become light...

Asotamâkêwin

Ancestral Reflection

Reflect on what you know about your ancestors and their experiences. What stories have been passed down through your family about their trials and triumphs? How do you connect with their legacy?

_____
_____
_____
_____
_____
_____
_____
_____
_____
_____
_____
_____
_____
_____
_____
_____
_____
_____

Asotamâkêwin

Asotamâkêwin

Asotamâkêwin

Embrace the complexities of your healing journey. Each twist, turn, and detour has contributed to your unique story.

Asotamâkêwin

Defining Moments

Write about key moments in your life when you first recognized the influence of intergenerational trauma. What experiences or realizations brought this to your awareness?

Asotamâkêwin

Asotamâkêwin

Asotamâkêwin

Take a moment to reflect on the milestones you've conquered, the lessons you've embraced, and the growth that has blossomed from the seeds of vulnerability.

Asotamâkêwin

Inherited Patterns

Explore patterns, behaviors, or beliefs that you've noticed in your family, which you suspect may be connected to intergenerational trauma. How have these patterns affected you, and how do you want to break them?

___

Asotamâkêwin

Asotamâkêwin

Asotamâkêwin

Healing is not linear; it is a continual, evolving process. Embrace the ebb and flow, and grant yourself the kindness and compassion you so willingly share with others.

Asotamâkêwin

Healing Rituals

Share any rituals or practices you've developed to honor your ancestors and promote healing. What activities or ceremonies help you connect with your past and heal from it?

_____
_____
_____
_____
_____
_____
_____
_____
_____
_____
_____
_____
_____
_____
_____
_____
_____

Asotamâkêwin

Asotamâkêwin

Asotamâkêwin

Acknowledge the strength it takes to navigate the shadows and the light. Every step forward, no matter how small, is a victory.

Asotamâkêwin

Lessons from Ancestors

Imagine having a conversation with an ancestor who experienced trauma. What wisdom or guidance do you think they would offer you on your own healing journey?

Asotamâkêwin

Asotamâkêwin

Asotamâkêwin

Your path is a testament to strength, courage, and the transformative nature of your spirit.

Asotamâkêwin

Generational Strength

Reflect on the strengths you've inherited from your ancestors. How have these qualities helped you overcome challenges in your life?

Asotamâkêwin

Asotamâkêwin

Asotamâkêwin

Use these pages to express your triumphs and challenges, your hopes and fears. Allow your words to braid together self-discovery, forgiveness, and healing.

Asotamâkêwin

Release & Forgiveness

Write a letter to yourself or to an ancestor, expressing forgiveness and letting go of any burdens or resentments related to intergenerational trauma. What does this act of forgiveness mean to you?

_____
_____
_____
_____
_____
_____
_____
_____
_____
_____
_____
_____
_____
_____
_____
_____
_____

Asotamâkêwin

Asotamâkêwin

Asotamâkêwin

Healing as Legacy

Consider the legacy you want to leave for future generations. How can your healing journey contribute to breaking the cycle of intergenerational trauma in your family?

_____
_____
_____
_____
_____
_____
_____
_____
_____
_____
_____
_____
_____
_____
_____
_____

Asotamâkêwin

Asotamâkêwin

Asotamâkêwin

Honoring Your Healing Journey

Asotamâkêwin

Self-Care Commitment

Outline specific self-care practices and commitments you will implement to support your ongoing healing journey. How will you prioritize self-care in your life?

_____
_____
_____
_____
_____
_____
_____
_____
_____
_____
_____
_____
_____
_____
_____

Asotamâkêwin

Asotamâkêwin

Asotamâkêwin

In this sacred space, we celebrate the resilience within you and honor the profound journey of healing you have undertaken.

Asotamâkêwin

Reflection on Growth

Reflect on your personal growth and insights gained through this journal.
How has the process of introspection and healing transformed you?

Asotamâkêwin

Asotamâkêwin

Asotamâkêwin

Asotamâkêwin

Asotamâkêwin

Asotamâkêwin

Asotamâkêwin

Asotamâkêwin

Asotamâkêwin

Asotamâkêwin

Asotamâkêwin

Asotamâkêwin

Asotamâkêwin

Asotamâkêwin

Asotamâkêwin

Asotamâkêwin

Asotamâkêwin

Asotamâkêwin

Asotamâkêwin

Asotamâkêwin

Asotamâkêwin

Asotamâkêwin

Asotamâkêwin

Asotamâkêwin

Asotamâkêwin

Asotamâkêwin

Asotamâkêwin

Asotamâkêwin

Asotamâkêwin

Asotamâkêwin

Asotamâkêwin

Asotamâkêwin

Asotamâkêwin

Asotamâkêwin

Asotamâkêwin

Asotamâkêwin

Asotamâkêwin

Asotamâkêwin

Asotamâkêwin

Asotamâkêwin

Asotamâkêwin

Asotamâkêwin

Asotamâkêwin

Asotamâkêwin

Asotamâkêwin

Bonus Material

Cutting-Edge Tools in Asotamâkêwin

Positive Visualization
Plant seeds of optimism by integrating daily positive visualization exercises.

Neuroplasticity
Cultivate a mindset of adaptability and growth by incorporating neuroplasticity-based activities into your daily routine.

Box Breathing
Powerful technique used to calm the mind, reduce stress, and enhance focus. It's a simple yet effective way to regain control over your breath and, consequently, your emotional state.

Nutrition & Detoxification
Understand that what you consume not only affects your physical health but also influences emotional, mental and spiritual well-being.
Intergenerational trauma leaves a mark, affecting our gut and influencing life's journey.
Our gut is a silent storyteller, holding the key to our emotional well-being.
Deep within our large intestine's microbiome, 95% of the neurotransmitters that shape our emotions are created—dopamine, serotonin, and the vital feel-good hormones.
When we heal our gut we heal the imprint of intergenerational trauma.
The uninvited guest to our dance called life.
Detoxification plays a crucial role in nutrition and holistic healing by aiding the body in eliminating toxins accumulated over time. This process ignites regeneration, purification, and paves the way for a legacy of vibrant health and empowerment for future generations.

*The guidance of a Certified Nutrition & Detoxification Educator is invaluable when it comes to navigating changes in your eating habits and proper detoxing protocols.
Your health is worth the expert advice.

Asotamâkêwin

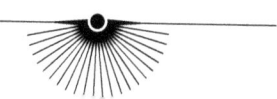

VISION BOARD

| Personal Goals | Health Goals | Big Dreams |

_____
_____
_____
_____
_____

| Your Why? | Your Why? | Your Why? |

_____
_____
_____
_____
_____

| Action Steps | Action Steps | Action Steps |

☐ _____
☐ _____
☐ _____
☐ _____
☐ _____

Asotamâkêwin

Asotamâkêwin

VISION BOARD

Personal Goals	Health Goals	Big Dreams
_____	_____	_____
_____	_____	_____
_____	_____	_____
_____	_____	_____
_____	_____	_____

Your Why?	Your Why?	Your Why?
_____	_____	_____
_____	_____	_____
_____	_____	_____
_____	_____	_____
_____	_____	_____

Action Steps	Action Steps	Action Steps
☐ _____	☐ _____	☐ _____
☐ _____	☐ _____	☐ _____
☐ _____	☐ _____	☐ _____
☐ _____	☐ _____	☐ _____
☐ _____	☐ _____	☐ _____

Asotamâkêwin

Asotamâkêwin

Self Care Ideas

Take a 10-minute mindful walk	Write down 3 things you are grateful for	Cook a healthy meal for yourself	Write down your Health Goals	Write a letter to your future self
Practice Box Breathing for 10 minutes	Connect with counseling support	Take a break from your mobile phone for the entire day	Try a new recipe	Take a long, relaxing bath
Visit a form of Mother Nature	Listen to your favorite music	Spend time with a pet	Gift a random act of kindness (Don't tell anyone)	Write down your Big Dreams
Write down your personal goals	Try a new hobby or revisit an old one	Research one of the Cutting Edge Tools in Asotamâkêwin	Daily Prayer-Meditation	Do something spontaneous
Buy yourself a small gift	Read a chapter of a book	Try a new tea or coffee flavor	Spend time in the sun	Write down 3 things you love about yourself
Practice gratitude while doing a daily task	Take the day off chores and errands	PSYCH-K	Do something creative	Reflect on the progress you've made this month

The final pages of this journal mark not just an end but a beginning.

Your story is an integral part of a collective consciousness.

Your unique narrative enriches our shared experiences.

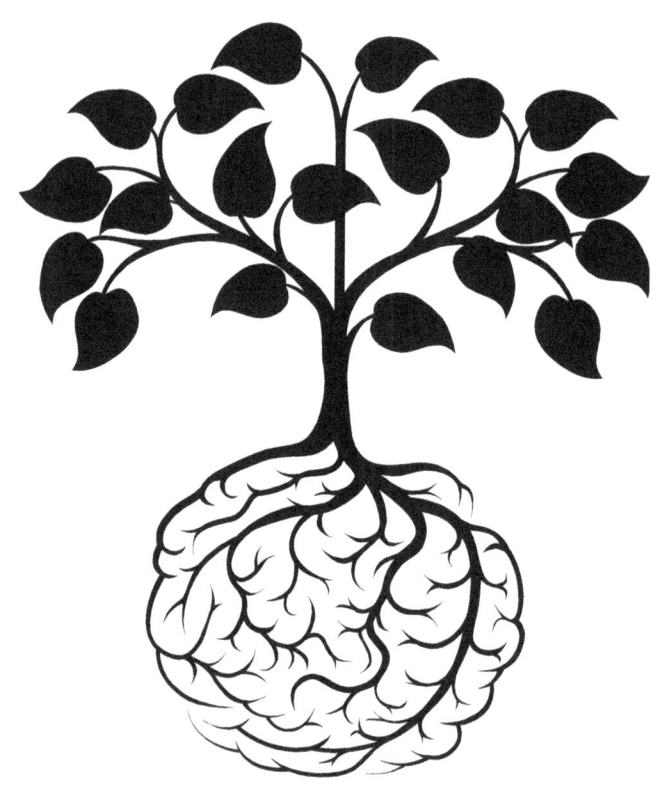

Be a lifelong learner

Unleash the ancestral wisdom within, speak life, create, connect with helpers, allies, healers, and arm yourself with knowledge that resonates with your spirit.

All my relations.

Asotamâkêwin

www.ingramcontent.com/pod-product-compliance
Lightning Source LLC
Chambersburg PA
CBHW080612170426
43209CB00007B/1406

Asotamâkêwin